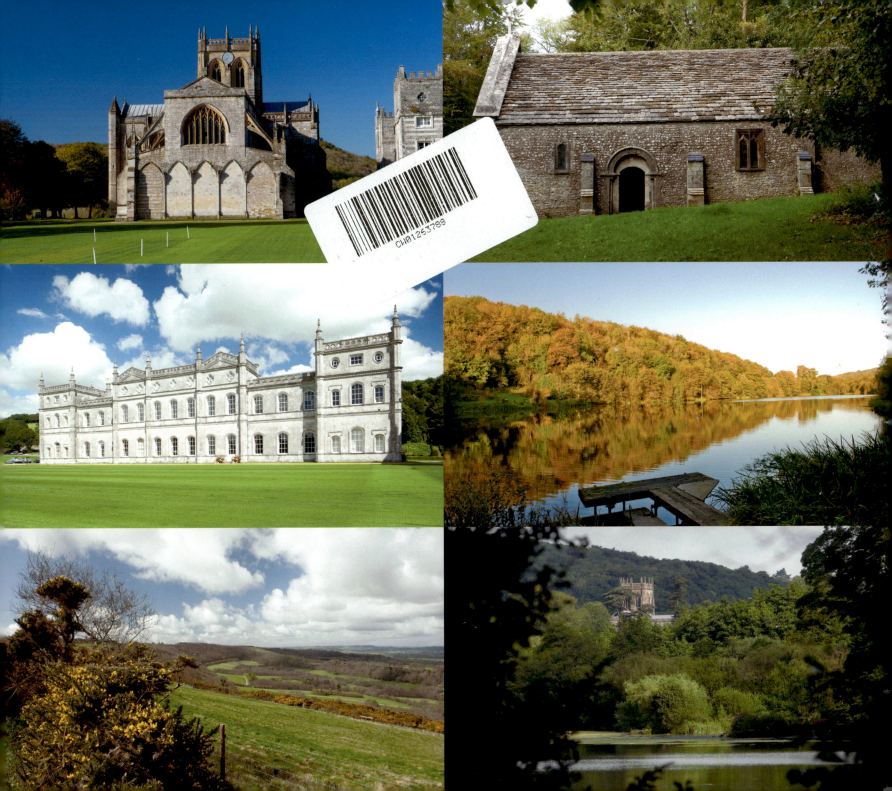

Copyright © 2013 Middleton Publishing

The photographs are by Daniel Rushall

Text by Michael McAvoy, with contributions from Martin Pook

Aerial photograph by Anthony Shearn

Photographs of the Street Fair by Peter Chafer and Valerie Downes

Historical advice by Chris Fookes

Designed by John Hawkins

Edited by Peta Nightingale

Portrait of a Village
Milton Abbas

The main street of the village of Milton Abbas lies in a thickly-wooded valley, known as Luccombe Bottom. To the North West is Milton Abbey, standing within a natural amphitheatre among rolling hills, where it has stood for over a thousand years. It is an idyllic area of the countryside, a beautiful, peaceful village that seems to embrace a bygone age. Today it is a thriving community but the previous centuries saw a certain amount of upheaval.

▶ St James Church and Cottage in Spring time

▶ Milton House (right) was originally the doctor's house and surgery

▶ No 33 (left) was the Old Black Horse in the 19th century

◀ Dale Cottage
▲ TOP The Hambro Arms   ▲ ABOVE The Post Office
▶ The former Tailors' Cottage (right) and the former Blacksmith's Cottage (left)

The Beginning – King Athelstan and the Monastic Period

The Abbey church was founded in 934 by King Athelstan (pictured on the right), although stories conflict as to why. One suggests that Athelstan was responsible for the death of his brother, who he thought was plotting to take the throne. He had him cast adrift at sea in a boat with neither oars nor sail, but was then consumed with guilt and built the church as a penance. A second legend has it that King Athelstan had a vision while camping on the site of St Catherine's Chapel on the hill east of the Abbey. In the vision he defeated the Danes in a coming battle, and then founded the church in gratitude when this came true.

Thirty years later, King Edgar, impressed by the revival of monasticism in England under St Dunstan, sacked the secular priests and replaced them with Benedictine monks. The monastery appears to have grown in importance during the Norman period, and a market town called Middleton grew up around the Abbey, thriving for well over 700 years. With a weekly market and an annual three-day fair granted by a charter from King Henry III in 1252, it was an important point on the route between Blandford and Dorchester.

Key Dates

- 934 Founding of the Abbey church by King Athelstan
- 1309 Church destroyed by fire, rebuilding commences after a few years
- 1540 Purchase by John Tregonwell, after Dissolution of the Monasteries
- 1752 Abbey and estates sold to Joseph Damer (later Lord Milton)
- 1773-79 The new village of Milton Abbas is created
- 1852 Estate purchased by Baron Hambro
- 1932 Estate sold by auction
- 1933 The Abbey purchased by the Diocese of Salisbury
- 1954 Milton Abbey school founded

St Catherine's Chapel

In the late 1100s the monks built St Catherine's Chapel on a hill looking down on the Abbey. St Catherine is a popular saint commonly associated with churches on hilltops; she was martyred in Alexandria and her body then taken by angels to the summit of Mount Sinai where her monastery still stands. Built as a pilgrim chapel, it is a beautifully simple Norman building, with a set of grass steps leading up from the Abbey 300 feet below.

◀ TOP Engraving by Marian Edwards c.1860
◀ BOTTOM The chapel today
▼ The interior

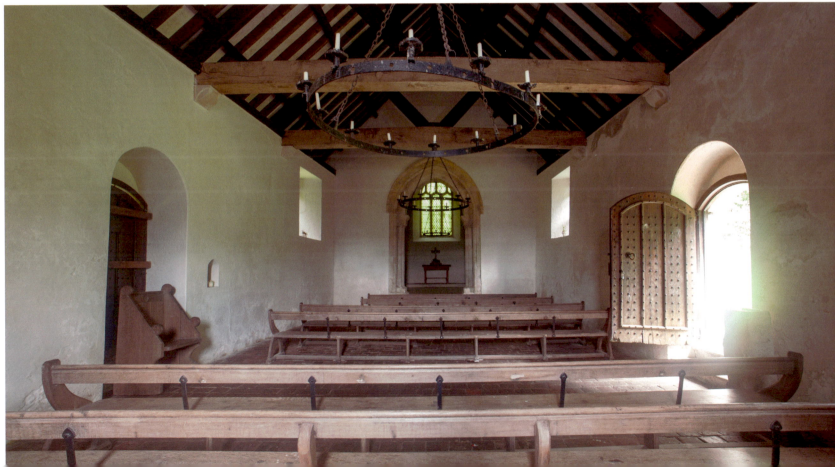

◄ The Abbey from St Catherine's Chapel

► The grass steps

Abbot Middleton

In 1309 there was a catastrophic fire, caused by a lightning strike on the spire of the Abbey church. Building work on a replacement of a larger scale began almost immediately, but was lengthy and sporadic and the new Abbey only reached its present size under Abbot William Middleton who was elected in 1482. He oversaw the Abbey until 1525 and was responsible for major work in rebuilding and adornment of the church. He is commemorated by a shield with his initial, held by an angel, located in the Abbot's Hall.

All this came to an end in 1539 with Henry VIII's Dissolution of the Monasteries. The monks were sent away and the Abbey's estates sold off.

▶ The shield commemorating Abbot Middleton in the Abbot's Hall

◀ The Abbot's Hall – completed in 1498; the sole remaining part of the original monastic buildings. Copyright Victoria and Albert Museum, London

The Tregonwell Era

John Tregonwell, a lawyer who had assisted Henry VIII in obtaining his divorce from Catherine of Aragon, accepted the surrender of the abbey and its lands on behalf of the King in 1539. Subsequently he bought the abbey and some of its estates, which remained in the Tregonwell family for more than two hundred years. Sir John died in 1565.

History relates a remarkable tale about John Tregonwell's great-grandson John in 1605. His nanny had taken him up the spiral staircase to the roof of the Abbey in the south-west corner. There he apparently leant over the low parapet to pick a rose growing on the wall below, but lost his balance and fell sixty feet to the ground. His distraught nanny rushed down to find the boy picking daisies on the lawn. It seems that the pinafore dress that was the vogue for boys at the time had acted as a parachute and saved his life.

▲ Milton Abbey in 1733 – engraving by Samuel and Nathaniel Buck showing the Abbey buildings before Damer's purchase in 1752 and the reconstruction that followed. On the right there is a glimpse of the old town of Middleton.

◀ FAR LEFT Sir John Tregonwell, by Henry Meyer, after Hans Holbein the Younger, copyright National Portrait Gallery, London
◀ LEFT Purbeck marble monument to Sir John Tregonwell

The Damer Era

In 1752 the Abbey and estates were sold to Joseph Damer, who later became Lord Milton. He disliked the old town of Middleton, wanting instead to create a mansion and grounds suitable to his standing. The celebrated landscape gardener Lancelot 'Capability' Brown was enlisted in 1764 to design the grounds, which would mean the removal of the town. After years of struggle with the townspeople, he was eventually successful in moving the grammar school to Blandford, pulling down the old town and relocating it in what is now known as Milton Abbas.

Building in the new model village began in the late 1770s. There is only one building that remains from the old town and that is Green Walk Cottage; in addition, the Almshouses that were built and endowed by John Tregonwell in 1674 were dismantled and rebuilt in the new village in 1779 and can be seen today.

Lord Milton also pulled down the tithe barn that was part of the old Abbey farmyard, and beams and materials from this were used in construction of the new village and in particular the new church.

▲ Engraving by Edward Rooker, c.1770. Initially, Lord Milton employed John Vardy as architect for his own grand mansion, but when Vardy died in 1765, he instructed the eminent architect Sir William Chambers to design a new mansion in the gothic style to blend with the Abbey church. It was not long before the two men fell out, the architect referring to his client as '…this imperious lord'. Chambers resigned and was replaced by James Wyatt who finished the house and designed most of the superb interior.

◀ TOP LEFT AND BELOW The Damer Monument, by Carlini, designed by Robert Adam, depicting Joseph Damer mourning his wife Caroline, 1775
◀ TOP RIGHT Portrait of Joseph Damer by Pompeo Batoni (private collection)

▲ Engraving by J. Hassell, 1801 ▶ The Abbey from the South West

▲ The Abbey from the Hilton Road. By the time of Lord Milton's death in 1798, the mansion was complete, as were the new village and the landscape work on the grounds, although it would be some years before the full effects of Brown's designs, including hundreds of acres of woodland would be seen to their full effect. The estates were passed on to several other family members, with varying degrees of success, and were then sold in 1852 to a Danish merchant banker, Charles Joachim, Baron Hambro.

▲ The choir and screen below the Eastern arch of the tower
◄ The interior looking towards the high altar and reredos

► The North transept – below the window is Carlini's monument to Lady Milton
► FAR RIGHT The Jesse window, designed by Augustus Pugin and made by John Hardman in 1847

The Mansion

◀ The main entrance of the mansion, which became the school, Milton Abbey, in 1954
▶ The exterior of the Abbot's Hall, at the rear of the mansion
▼ BELOW The Kings Room
▼ BOTTOM The inner courtyard

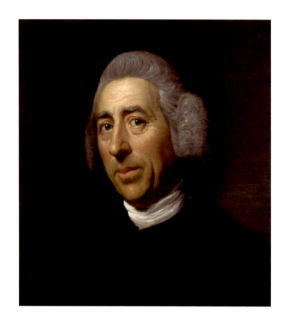

Capability Brown

From 1763, Capability Brown worked on the estate and designed the setting for the mansion and the Abbey. His scheme included the planting of woods on the surrounding hills and the result was an idyllic landscape, rated as one of Brown's best in England.

The lake was conceived by Brown as part of his grand landscape scheme, replacing the former lake close to the Abbey. His original idea was to extend the ornamental lake down the length of the valley to the front of the Abbey, but this was later abandoned as too ambitious a plan.

▲ Delcombe Valley
◄ Green Walk Cottage – the only remaining building of the old town of Middleton. It is located by the grass steps, leading to St Catherine's Chapel.

▲ A gate pillar of the original main entrance to the Abbey

◄ The valley linking the lake to the Abbey

The Village

▲ Engraving of the village of Milton Abbas, c.1851 copyright RIBA Library, Books & Periodicals

▶ The village street, an engraving by Marian Edwards, c. 1860

▲ An assortment of cottage doors

◄ The village street seen from across the lake

▲ The Almshouses were built and endowed by John Tregonwell in the old town of Middleton in 1674. The building is the original, which was dismantled and reconstructed in the new village and completed in 1779.

▶ The Old Rectory, probably designed by Sir William Chambers and built c.1780. The vicar of Milton Abbas lived here until 1955.

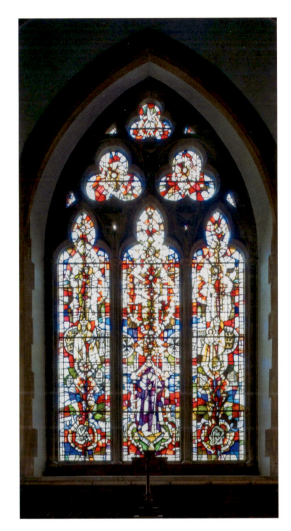  

▲ LEFT East window, which was designed and made by Lawrence Lee in 1969
MIDDLE The font, in the entrance porch. This was moved from the Abbey church
RIGHT The War Memorial, which records the names of those who fell in both World Wars

◄ St James Church was designed by James Wyatt, and constructed of timbers and stone from the abbey tithe barn that was part of the old Abbey farmyard and was pulled down on the instructions of Lord Milton. The new church was consecrated in 1786, twelve years after building work began.

▶ Portrait of Carl Joachim Hambro, artist unknown

▶ OPPOSITE The entrance to the Abbey, added in 1865 during Sir Gilbert Scott's restoration

▼ The Hambro tomb

The Hambro Era

The Abbey church had fallen into a poor state of repair and Hambro retained the services of Sir George Gilbert Scott to carry out a complete restoration, saving it from potential ruin. Through their eighty years at Milton Abbey Baron Hambro and his son Everard oversaw a period of peace and prosperity. They provided a hospital and doctor in the village, and piped water in from an artesian bore at the north end of the lake. This was then pumped to a reservoir in the woods behind the village from whence it gravitated to a series of standpipes in the street. The Baron died in 1877.

The Baron's sons Charles and Sir Everard continued the good works in both the Abbey and the village. But by 1932 rents from agricultural holdings, which formed the majority of the tenancies, had fallen to abysmal levels and the Hambros put the house and estates on the market. No buyer was found for the whole, so individual farmers, cottagers and others bought up property and became landowners for the first time. The house and Abbey were eventually sold to the Ecclesiastical Commissioners with a view to establishing a theological college. This was not to be and the Abbey church was sold to the Diocese of Salisbury and the mansion was used for a while as a faith healing centre, before being sold in 1953 to establish a public school, Milton Abbey, which continues to thrive in Lord Milton's mansion.

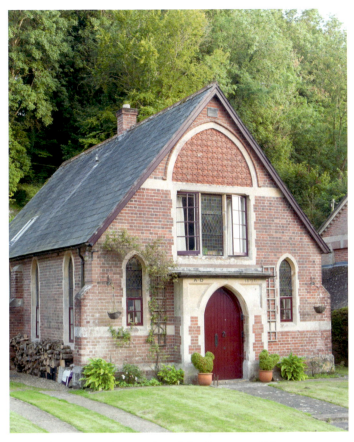

▲ The former Wesleyan Chapel, built in 1895/6 on the site of the old workhouse. The chapel closed in 1970 and is now a private house.

▶ TOP Lake Lodge, formerly a lodge to the park, constructed in the mid-19th century.

▶ BELOW The former village school was built in about 1860 by Baron Hambro, for 150 children. It closed in 2005 and is now a private house.

◀ The former Cottage Hospital, opened in 1873, endowed by the Hambro family, and closed as a hospital in 1937. It is now a private house.

Post Second World War

A view of Catherine's Well, houses that were built after the Second World War to the North of the village. The area expanded further in the 1960s and 1990s.

Local landscape

◄ Bulbarrow Hill, which overlooks the Blackmore Vale

▼ The lake from the jetty

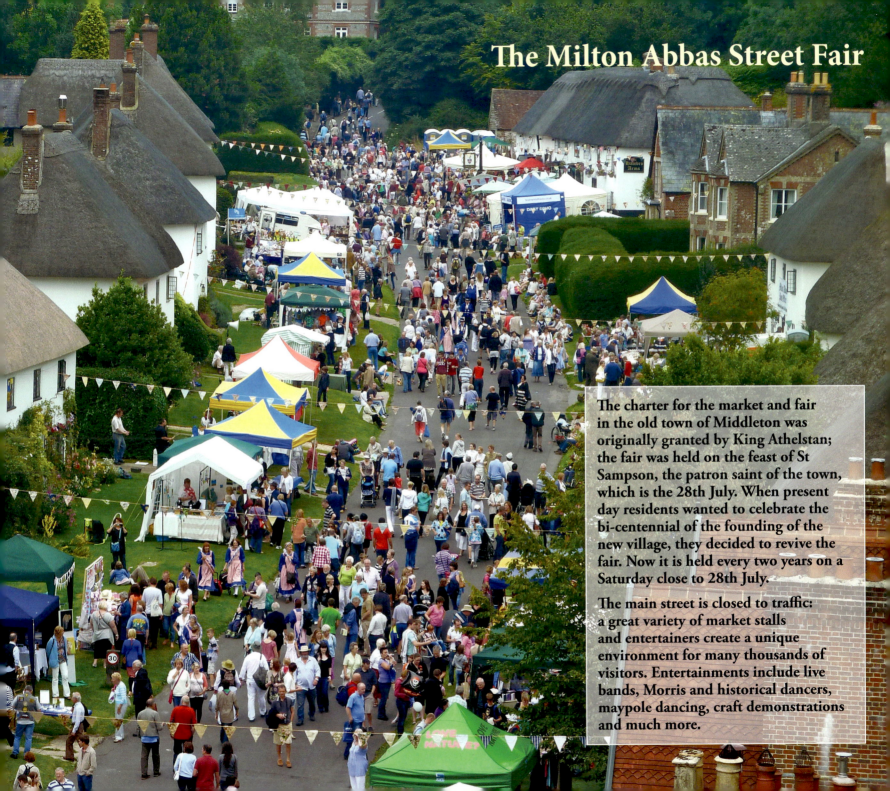

The Milton Abbas Street Fair

The charter for the market and fair in the old town of Middleton was originally granted by King Athelstan; the fair was held on the feast of St Sampson, the patron saint of the town, which is the 28th July. When present day residents wanted to celebrate the bi-centennial of the founding of the new village, they decided to revive the fair. Now it is held every two years on a Saturday close to 28th July.

The main street is closed to traffic: a great variety of market stalls and entertainers create a unique environment for many thousands of visitors. Entertainments include live bands, Morris and historical dancers, maypole dancing, craft demonstrations and much more.